TEST YOUR

MW01488906

Punctuation

Boswell Taylor

Headway · Hodder & Stoughton

Notes for Parents and Teachers

This is a work book. In the main part of the book each double page is concerned with one of the elements of punctuation. The rule is given, usually with examples, and exercises follow. The Answers at the end of the book are provided for the special tests which are prefaced with ★ Now test yourself. The Story section provides general practice in the use of punctuation.

We use punctuation every time we speak. We need the code of punctuation marks when we write to help the reader to understand the meaning better. People vary in the way they use punctuation marks. As with the English language, there is nothing fixed and final in the use of punctuation. There is a tendency today to use less punctuation than our parents did. Some computers do not use some of the punctuation marks at all. There are few golden rules. The one question we should ask ourselves is: Have we made our meaning clear?

This book explains what the punctuation marks are, their value, and how they are usually used. The exercises should consolidate the instruction. It is an advantage if the work can be read aloud. The punctuation should help to make the reading fluent and the meaning plain.

Contents

Why we need punctuation

When we talk we can do all kinds of things to make our meaning clear. We can put words into groups or separate them. We can pause for breath or effect. We can emphasize words or phrases to make them sound important. We can raise our voices to indicate that we are asking a question. We can express our feelings by exclaiming with joy or surprise or fright.

We can do none of these things when we write. We therefore use a code to make our meaning clear. The code tells the reader *how* to read the words we have written. This code is called punctuation. The code signs are called punctuation marks. These are the code signs. These are the punctuation marks:

.	,	?	!	,
full stop or period	comma	question mark	exclamation mark	apostrophe
—	:	;	-	( )
dash	colon	semi-colon	hyphen	brackets

" "   or   , ,

quotation marks or inverted commas or speech marks or lip marks

You will find these punctuation marks in letters. You will find them in books. You will see them in this book. You will see them on television screens. You will find them nearly everywhere that you can see words. Without written marks of punctuation to replace speech signals, we could not connect, emphasize, or separate our thoughts in any intelligible way. Punctuation marks help the reader to understand our ideas. Without these marks no clear writing is possible. Punctuation marks can give a different meaning to the words in a sentence. Look at this sentence:

What are we waiting for Susan?

This is one meaning . . .	What are we waiting for, Susan?
Change the punctuation marks and we have another meaning . . .	What! Are we waiting for Susan?
Again . . .	What are we waiting for? Susan.

The punctuation code is essential to reading aloud. Try reading aloud what you have written, and then you will know if the punctuation has made your meaning clear.

A sentence begins with a capital and ends with a full stop.

The full stop (or period) is the punctuation mark most frequently used.
A full stop is necessary when a speaker stops for breath.
It brings a statement or a single idea to an end.

Punctuate the following. Begin each sentence with a capital letter.
End each sentence with a full stop.
Note that the first one is done for you. (This rule applies to each exercise in the book.)

A1   the cowboy was thrown from his horse

   .The .cowboy .was .thrown .from .his .horse. . . . .

  2   she climbed the mountain to its snow-capped summit

       . . . .

  3   rockets shot into the sky

       . . . .

  4   we are going to the fair

       . . . .

  5   the tiger leapt upon the back of the frightened animal

       . . . .

  6   the space-craft landed on the moon

       . . . .

Six sentences have been split up. Here are their endings.
   netted the floundering salmon   looped the loop
   hit the ball into the air   painted a picture of the barn
   reached the sunken wreck   skidded round the corner

Give the correct ending for each beginning shown below.

B1 The impatient batsman *hit. the. ball. into. the. air.* . . . .

  2 The fisherman . . . .

  3 The diver . . . .

  4 The motor-cyclist . . . .

  5 The brave pilot . . . .

  6 The artist . . . .

Full stops are used in abbreviations

Abbreviations are the shortened form of words or phrases. They often consist of the initial letters of the words in the phrases.

Use full stops after initials in names. Write the initials only of the first names.

A 1 Frederick George Smith   Susan Joanne Edmunds

     F. G. Smith ....   *S. J. Edmunds* ....

   2 Write your own name in its abbreviated form.

       ....

   3 Write the abbreviated names of three people you know.

       ....

Full stops are placed after some abbreviations.
These are abbreviations.

    C.O.D.   Nov.   H.M.S.   V.C.   G.P.O.   Co.   v.   cr.

Write the following as abbreviations.

B 1 Trades Union Congress . *T.U.C.*   2 Bachelor of Science ....

   3 December ....   4 Her Royal Highness ....

   5 United States of America ......   6 Royal Naval Reserve ....

   7 versus ....   8 Cash on delivery ....

   9 credit ....   10 Victoria Cross ....

For what words or phrases are these the abbreviations?

C 1 G.P.O. *General Post office* ...... 2 Nov. ....

   3 H.M.S. .... 4 Co. ....

There is no rule because so many abbreviations have lost their stops. BBC, LBW, BR, AA have lost their full stops. What do these abbreviations stand for? Mathematical and scientific terms are often written without stops. Examples are 4th, cm, per cent. What do these stand for?
Contractions which include the last letter of the original word do not have stops. Dr, Mr, Bros and St are examples. Can you find more?

Write the following as abbreviations.

D 1 British Broadcasting   2 millimetres ....
     Corporation ... *BBC* ....

   3 Member of Parliament .... 4 Justice of the Peace ....

How to use capital letters

Capital letters are used to begin sentences.

Punctuate these instructions. Write in sentences using full stops and capital letters. There are five sentences.

A   ask a friend to hold a coin in his or her hand tightly inform your friend that you can tell the day's date put your hand on his or her head pretend to think hard tell your friend today's date

Ask a friend to hold a coin in his or her hand tightly. . . . .

. . . .

. . . .

. . . .

. . . .

. . . .

Capital letters are used to begin special names.
Write names which are examples of the following.

B 1 king   president   admiral
     Arthur . . . .

  2 ship   pop group   horse
     H.M.S. Victory . . .   .

  3 country   continent   city
     France . . . .

  4 mountain   river   desert
     Snowdon . . . .

Capital letters are used for 'I' (capital 'i') and to begin words in titles.
Write titles which are examples of the following.

C 1 an adventure book . . . *The Thirty-nine Steps* . . . .

  2 a national anthem . . . .

  3 a folk song . . . .

  4 a pop song . . . .

  5 a poem . . . .

  6 a television, radio or theatre play . . . .

. . . .

Capital letters are used to begin direct speech and lines of poetry.

6

★ Now test yourself (capitals and full stops)

Punctuate the sentences in A and B using the capital letter and the full stop.

A 1 the dog barked when the burglar approached

. . . .

2 as he passed through the laser beam the gates shut

. . . .

3 no one knew the answer

. . . .

4 the horseman was lost in a cloud of dust

. . . .

B the prized mascot of an american regiment in germany was a buffalo named cross-eyes they kept it in a large cage a british regiment felt sorry for the animal one morning the buffalo disappeared in its place was an oxo cube

. . . .

. . . .

. . . .

. . . .

. . . .

C Write this verse in five lines adding capital letters and full stops where necessary.
there was an old man of kildare, who climbed into a very high chair; when he said, "here i stays, till the end of my days", that immovable man of kildare

. . . .

. . . .

. . . .

. . . .

. . . .

(Answers on page 30)

7

A comma marks a brief pause in a sentence

The insertion of commas can change the meaning of a sentence.

Fiona, my friend, is riding the horse. (Fiona is riding the horse.)
Fiona, my friend is riding the horse. (Fiona is not riding the horse.)

Insert the commas in these sentences to give the meaning intended.

A 1 Carpet for sale, the property of a lady, too large for her house.
  2 The woman was killed while cooking the dinner in a frightful way.
  3 Wanted: piano for a lady with a patterned front and mahogany legs.
  4 The clown who knew the girl wore patched trousers and had a red nose.
  5 The mother bought a comb for the baby with plastic teeth.

In this sentence the comma has been inserted *in the wrong place*.
Rewrite the sentence correctly, with two commas.

  6 The Earl who was the chieftain of his clan wore nothing, to show his rank.

Commas are used to separate names in a list:
Children go to school on Monday, Tuesday, Wednesday, Thursday and Friday.
Or we can write this.
Children go to school on Monday, Tuesday, Wednesday, Thursday, and Friday.

In the first example we have omitted the final comma.

Answer the following questions in sentences, choosing the correct items from each list.

B 1 Which three are birds?   wrens, robins, zebras, fawns, swifts
    Wrens, robins and swifts are birds. . . . .
  2 Which three are flowers?   roses, pearls, whelks, pinks, asters
    . . . .
  3 Which three are furniture?   tables, attics, divans, anoraks, mirrors
    . . . .
  4 Which three are fruits?   apricots, goblets, pears, tangos, plums
    . . . .
  5 Which three are drinks?   nectarine, milk, chocolate, wagtail, coffee
    . . . .

Commas may be used to separate a sequence of actions or instructions.

Climb the hill, cross the river, walk along the lane, and you will reach the farm.

★ Now test yourself (commas)

Punctuate the following, inserting commas where necessary.

A 1 The farther he travelled the more weary he became.
  2 I will go but you will stay here.
  3 The deeper you dig however the wetter the ground becomes.
  4 Before the fire brigade arrived the house was burnt to the ground.
  5 First I would like to know which school you attend.
  6 Yes I am much better today.
  7 Jane Powell my best friend will be there to meet me.
  8 Stand in front of me Jonathan and let me take a good look at you.
  9 The prisoner wounded though he was managed to escape.
 10 There are 5 2 6 7 8 3 9 1 people living in the country.

Answer the following questions in sentences. Choose the correct items.

B 1 Which three are towns?   Manchester, Vietnam, Bonn, Oslo, Sweden

. . . .

  2 Which three are games?   chess, granite, lacrosse, boogie-woogie, tennis

. . . .

  3 Which three are insects?   ant, earwig, weasel, eel, termite

. . . .

  4 Which three are instruments?   barometer, clutch, camera, computer, buoy

. . . .

  5 Which three are minerals?   sonata, zinc, iron, tungsten, migraine

. . . .

To help you   Commas are used to help the reader, not to confuse him or her. They indicate a pause or a change in the expression or tone of voice. Try reading the sentences aloud (or nearly so) noting when you pause or change your tone of voice.
There is a tendency for fewer commas to be used nowadays, but they should always be used if they help the reader by making the meaning clearer.

NOTE   We use commas to divide numbers (5,683,542) but not in dates (1983). In high numbers we sometimes use a space instead of a comma.

When to use the question mark (?)

When we ask a question we use a special tone of voice.
When we write a question we use a question mark (?).
A question usually expects an answer.

The question mark is used only when an actual direct question is asked.

What is your name?   When will you be able to go?

Write answers to these questions.

A 1 When do leaves fall from trees?

Leaves fall . *in the autumn.* . . . .

2 Where do rooks build their nests?

Rooks build . . . .

3 Why does a hedgehog have prickles?

A hedgehog has . . . .

4 Which animal has tusks and a trunk?

. . . . has tusks and a trunk.

5 How does a cricket chirp?

A cricket chirps by . . . .

6 What is the favourite food of the squirrel?

The favourite food. . . . .

Write questions which could give these answers.

B 1 . . *What time does the bus leave?* . . . .

The bus leaves at noon.

2 . . . .

The kiwi lives in New Zealand.

3 . . . .

Paris is the capital of France.

4 . . . .

The disco is held on Thursday evenings.

Questions often begin with What. . .? When. . .? Why. . .? Where. . .?
How. . .?
Use the question mark after a single word that indicates a question.
Why?   How?   Where?   When?   What?

The question mark is used after a statement followed by a short question.

It never rains but it pours, does it?

Notice the comma before the question.

Add the short questions appropriate to the following statements.

A 1 You are not the tallest girl in the class, . *are you?* . . . .

2 April is not the wettest month, ...

3 You can't grow onions in mud, ...

4 We will not climb to the top of the mountain, ...

5 You will try harder next time, ...

6 It's cold outside, ...

This is the report you gave to the police after you escaped from a gang of kidnappers. Write down the actual questions you were asked.

The gang asked me my nationality. They wanted to know my name. They asked me why I was visiting the island. They wanted to know how much money I had. They asked if my father was rich. They asked if he would pay a ransom for me.

B 1 . . *What is your nationality?* . . . .

2 . . . .

3 . . . .

4 . . . .

5 . . . .

6 . . . .

Punctuate the following.

C 1 SON   Dad☐what has a black and red striped body☐two great eyes on stalks☐six hairy legs and a long proboscis☐

FATHER   I don't know☐Why☐

SON   One has just settled on your bald patch☐

2 LADY   Do you charge for bread☐

WAITER   No☐

LADY   Do you charge for gravy☐

WAITER   No☐

LADY   May I have two slices of bread with gravy☐please☐

How to use the exclamation mark (!)

The exclamation mark (!) should be used with caution. Well selected words can often do the same job. A spatter of exclamation marks on a page will irritate a reader. If in doubt – miss out.

The exclamation mark is used to express strong or sudden feelings.
Help!   Good for you!   Oh!   That hurts!

It can be used to emphasize a command or a strong viewpoint.
Go away!   Attention!   I don't want to talk about it!

It can be used to show irony, sarcasm or amusement.
What a funny girl you are!   You are the last one to talk about envy!

Exclamation marks can follow sentences, words or phrases. The next word always begins with a capital letter.

Punctuate, inserting an exclamation mark or a question mark, or both.

A 1 Oh dear are you going away

Oh dear! Are you going away? . . . .

2 Help it burns where is the ointment

. . . .

3 Get off the grass can't you see that it is wet

. . . .

4 Jump to it do you think you are the only person who wants to try

. . . .

5 Stop it I don't want to hear anything about it

. . . .

6 Let go what do you think you are doing I won't stop

. . . .

Punctuate with one full stop, one question mark and two exclamation marks.

B   ''My dog's got no nose☐''
     ''Poor dog☐How does he smell☐''
     ''Awful☐''

★ Now test yourself (question marks and exclamation marks)

Punctuate the following, inserting question marks and exclamation marks.

1 Where did you find the owl with the broken wing

. . . .

2 Don't make me laugh

. . . .

3 You are the most remarkable person I have ever met

. . . .

4 Am I invited to your Party Do you really want me to come

. . . .

5 Will you come to me immediately I said immediately

. . . .

6 Oh Why did you creep so quietly up to me You are frightening

. . . .

7 Dear Dear Why don't you hit the nail instead of my finger

. . . .

8 Goodness gracious me Look at the time Shouldn't we be going

. . . .

9 Knock Knock Who's there

. . . .

10 What are you doing That hurts

. . . .

11 Where are you hiding Come out at once

. . . .

12 Now Now You have forgotten

. . . .

To help you   The question mark and the exclamation mark suggest a tone of voice. Try reading the sentences aloud. Question marks are only used when a direct question is asked. Do not over-use exclamation marks. Ration them.

How to use quotation marks ('' '' or ' ')

Quotation marks are sometimes single (' '), and sometimes double ('' '').

They are sometimes called inverted commas, speech marks or lip marks.

Quotation marks indicate the actual (and exact) words spoken or quoted.

''The pirates will all hang,'' said the captain.

The captain said, ''The pirates will all hang.''

Notice the comma separating the actual words spoken from the rest.

Quotation marks go round each part of a direct quotation if it is broken up.

''The pirates,'' said the captain, ''will all hang.''

Notice the commas separating the actual words spoken from the rest:

,'' said the captain, ''

Notice also that, as the quotation is a broken sentence, the second part does not begin with a capital letter.

The quotation may consist of more than one sentence.

''The pirates will all hang,'' said the captain. ''They are all criminals. They have killed many sailors. They must die.''

Punctuate the following using quotation marks. All the other kinds of punctuation are given.

A 1 Oh dear! I have lost my way, said the instructor, and I don't know which way to go.

"Oh dear! I have lost my way," said the instructor,
"and I don't know which way to go."

2 I hit the ball over the wall, said the boy, and we can't find it.

. . . .

. . . .

3 Stop that thief! cried the old lady.

. . . .

4 Kate said firmly, I want my banana now, Grannie.

. . . .

5 Ah! I think I know you now said the barber. Aren't you the man who gave me a dud tenpenny piece?

. . . .

. . . .

14

Punctuate the following using quotation marks.
The other kinds of punctuation are given.

B 1 I have lost my memory,   said the patient.
      When did that happen?   asked the doctor.
      When did what happen?   said the patient.

   2 We have a hen,   said Jackie, that lays brown eggs.
      Well, what is so wonderful about that?   asked Meg.
      Could you do it?   asked Jackie.

   3 A boy was swimming in a private pool. The owner saw him and was
      very annoyed. He shouted to the boy,   You can't swim in this pool.
      It's private.   The boy answered,   I am not swimming. I am only
      trying to stop myself sinking.

These are reported conversations. Using quotation marks, write out the
actual words spoken.

C 1 Jerry asked Tom how he had got on in the milk-drinking competition.
      Tom answered that he had won by three laps.

      . . . .

      . . . .

      . . . .

      . . . .

   2 Mother said that Maggie knew that she must not eat with a knife.
      Maggie replied that she did know, but her fork leaked!

      . . . .

      . . . .

      . . . .

      . . . .

   3 Write a story of your own using quotation marks.

How to use the apostrophe 1

The apostrophe (') is used to show possession.
  John's bat = the bat that belongs to John
  Jilly's bike = the bike that belongs to Jilly

Rule One   In the singular (referring to only one owner) use the apostrophe + s.

Make the following possessive, using the apostrophe.

A 1 the spade of the gardener . . . *the gardener's spade* . . . .

  2 the cow of the farmer . . . .

  3 the tape-recorder of the teacher . . . .

  4 the ring of the bride . . . .

  5 the song of the thrush . . . .

  6 the engine of the car . . . .

Rule Two   In the plural (referring to more than one owner) add the apostrophe only *when the plural ends in ----s or -----es.*

B 1 the pencils of the boys . . . . . *the boys' pencils* . . . .

  2 the sails of the boats . . . .

  3 the bells of the churches . . . .

  4 the ears of the donkeys . . . .

  5 the shields of the squires . . . .

  6 the hats of the ladies . . . .

Rule Three   When the plural does not end in -s add the apostrophe + s.
C 1 the boots of the policemen . . *the policemen's boots* . . . .

  2 the anoraks of the men . . . .

  3 the homework of the children . . . .

  4 the jewels of the women . . . .

Caution   Some words showing possession *never* take an apostrophe.
They are
  its   hers   his   ours   yours   theirs

  The snake raised its head and showed its fangs. . . . . . .

D   Write a sentence for each of the words above, similar to the example.
   Do not use an apostrophe.

Write the following sentences making use of the apostrophe to show possession. The words to be changed are shown in mauve.

E 1 The coats of the ladies were taken to the cloakroom.

The ladies' coats were taken to the cloakroom.

2 The books were placed on the desk of the librarian.

. . . .

3 The mud was solid on the boots of the workmen.

. . . .

4 The head of my brother was bruised from the blow.

. . . .

5 The burglar broke into the house of Mr Charles.

. . . .

6 From the display the shop evidently sold the clothes of babies.

. . . .

7 The voices of women made themselves heard.

. . . .

8 The teacher was pleased with the interest of the parents.

. . . .

9 The family had a holiday of three months.

. . . .

10 Call at the shop of Brown and Smith on the way back.

. . . .

In the following sentences insert the correct pronouns from the list.
Do not insert apostrophes.   its   hers   his   ours   yours
    theirs

F 1 It is not ours; it is *theirs*.

2 Yours are red; . . . . are blue.

3 The tree sheds . . . . leaves in autumn.

4 The knight returned . . . . sword to the scabbard.

5 This is mine; . . . . is still lost.

How to use the apostrophe 2

The apostrophe (') is used to show that letters have been omitted when two (or more) words have been run together to make an abbreviation.

did not   didn't   we will   we'll   shall not   shan't

Abbreviate these phrases to make one word with an apostrophe in each case.

A 1 all is.... *all's* .....   2 you are ....   3 I am............

4 that is ....   5 there is ....   6 he is............

7 did not..........   8 does not ....   9 do not ....

10 would not ....   11 have not ....   12 should not.......

Abbreviate these phrases. You should omit more than one letter in each case.

B 1 you will .. *you'll* ...   2 will not ....   3 shall not ....

4 he would........   5 she will ....   6 I would ....

7 we have.........   8 I have..........   9 they will.........

10 who have ....   11 I will............   12 of the clock ....

Write these words as phrases of more than one word and without apostrophes.

C 1 can't . *can not* ....   2 it's ....   3 isn't............

4 I'd ....   5 he'd............   6 he'll ....

7 we've...........   8 they'll ....   9 we'll...........

10 she'll ....   11 won't...........   12 who's ....

13 whate'er ....   14 where'er ....   15 whoe'er.........

16 wasn't..........   17 daren't ....   18 mustn't ....

19 you've..........   20 we're...........   21 who've ....

22 sou'wester ....   23 o'clock..........   24 Hallowe'en.......

Abbreviations such as those shown above are used in speech and dialogue.
The words are usually written in full in formal and polite letters.
The full words, without the apostrophe, are usually used in text books and in fiction that is not in dialogue.

The *o* is used in *won't* because *wol* was the old form of *will*.
Use the apostrophe in *it's* only when it means *it is*.

Write the following sentences making use of the apostrophe as an abbreviation. The words to be changed are shown in mauve.

D 1 We will arrive at six of the clock.

. . . .

2 I am too clever and have not been trapped yet.

. . . .

3 Although it is time to go I will stay a little longer.

. . . .

4 All is well with us and that is as it should be.

. . . .

5 Now we have fallen off our bikes they will win.

. . . .

6 Wherever you go you will be recognised.

. . . .

7 There is nowhere you are welcome with that frown.

. . . .

8 We shall not know the result until morning.

. . . .

9 We do not want to go and we will not go.

. . . .

10 I shall not forget the way you have helped me.

. . . .

11 I would be delighted if you would keep the money.

. . . .

12 Where there is a will there is a way.

. . . .

13 Do not tell me you have lost your shorts.

. . . .

How to use hyphens — dashes — and brackets

The hyphen (-) is used to mark the division of a word at the end of a line: always divide a word only between syllables. Al-ways is an example.

Hyphens are used in some compound words. They separate or join the words.

Insert the hyphen in the following.

A 1 son-in-law   2 vice president   3 co operative
  4 Anglo Indian   5 mile long   6 old fashioned

Hyphens are used in numbers between 21 and 99, and in fractions.

B 1 thirty-four   2 seventy eight   3 twenty nine
  4 two thirds   5 three quarters   6 seven eighths

Dashes — which look like these — and brackets (which look like these) are used to show an aside in a sentence or for extra information to be given. A single dash may be used before an added thought at the end of a sentence.
Brackets (sometimes called parentheses) enclose information and are used in pairs.

Insert dashes — wherever necessary — in the following.

C 1 You may although I shall be surprised if you do enjoy this music.
  2 The 'Mary Rose' that noble ship sank before the eyes of the king.
  3 Jonathan Thomson if his brother cannot come will join us at the fair.
  4 The towels if they are not too wet will be used to sit on.
  5 I will try and I will go on trying until I succeed.
  6 The sharks were man-eaters or so I believed.

Insert brackets (parentheses) in the following. Enclose figures and references.

D 1 I used an axe a large one to split the wood.
  2 The stamp a small adhesive square was stuck to the document.
  3 One section in the book Chapter 2 describes the space craft.
  4 Can you let me have twenty-five 25 pounds?
  5 I will give you eleven 11 copies of the poem.
  6 The largest crater is about 700 miles 1100 kilometres wide.

How to use colons and semi-colons

The colon (:) is a mark of anticipation. It starts a list or introduces a quotation.

Insert the colon in the following.

A 1 Campers must bring these items: sleeping-bags, ground-sheets and food.
  2 These are capital cities Paris, Moscow, London and Vienna.
  3 The City of Birmingham has a motto Forward.
  4 Three motorways are closed M4, M1 and M5.
  5 Three drinks are served cocoa, coffee and coca cola.
  6 I have three favourite teams Aston Villa, Arsenal and Norwich.

A semi-colon marks a pause in a sentence. It is stronger than a comma; it is not as strong as a full stop. A semi-colon (;) may be used instead of a conjunction like 'and' or 'but'.
Insert the semi-colon in the following.

B 1 Look at the map; check the route.
  2 Sean works hard Jack plays all day long.
  3 The king smiled kindly at June one could see he was pleased.
  4 I will read the story when I come to the end you will know why.
  5 The brother was quieter he entered the world of his books.
  6 At noon I left everybody had left.

Sometimes a semi-colon is used after a group of words in a sentence.
Insert the semi-colons in the following.

C 1 Sirens blared; bells rang; whistles shrieked; and people cheered.
  2 The engine spluttered it stopped it started again then it stopped completely.
  3 The prisoner jumped the wall he ran across the field he disappeared.

A semi-colon is used between items which contain commas.
Insert the semi-colons in the following.

D 1 The group consisted of three girls: Joan, first guitarist; Jane, second guitarist; and Jacqueline, drummer.
  2 Three boys were key players: Darren, striker Peter, goalkeeper and Sam, sweeper.

★Now test yourself

Punctuate the following. The punctuation marks you need are shown on the right.
Cross out each mark as you use it. You should use these and no more.

1	MOTHER:	"Don't pull faces at the bull-dog."	″″″″″″
	SON:	"But, mother, he began it!"	″″″″″″!
2	PATIENT:	What can you give me for my flat feet	″″?
	DOCTOR:	What about a foot pump	″″-!
3	ONLOOKER:	Why are you rolling the potato patch	″″?
	GARDENER	I m trying to grow mashed potatoes	″″′.
4	DINER:	What has happened to this egg	″″?
	WAITRESS:	I don t know madam I only laid the table	″″′,,.
5	DINER:	Do you serve ducklings here	″″?
	WAITER:	We serve anybody sir Sit down	″″,.!
6	STUDENT:	How do you make a sausage roll	″″?
	FRIEND:	That s easy Just turn it over and over	″″′!.
7	FATHER:	How do you know your teacher loves you	″″?
	GIRL:	She puts wee kisses next to each sum I do There	″″!.
8	PATIENT:	Doctor I feel as limp as a pair of curtains	″″,.
	DOCTOR:	You had better pull yourself together then	″″.
9	SHOPPER:	I don t like the look of that codfish It s bad	″″′.!′
	FISHMONGER:	If it s looks you want why not buy a goldfish	″″′,?
10	VICAR:	Your brother is very small isn t he	″″,′?
	BOY:	Well vicar you see he is only my half brother	″″,,,,-
11	CUSTOMER:	This is a second hand shop isn t it	″″-,′?
	ASSISTANT:	Yes	″″.
	CUSTOMER:	That s lucky Please fit one on my watch	″″′!.
12	FRIEND:	So you ve lost your dog Why don t you advertise	″″′.′?
	DOG-OWNER:	Don t be silly My dog can t read	″″′!′.

13	BROTHER:	Well Jean how do you like school	" " , , ?
	SISTER:	Closed	" " !
14	GRETA:	I ve changed my mind	" " '.
	CLARE:	Does the new mind work any better	" " ?
15	MOTHER:	Have you filled the salt cellar yet Nesta	" " , ?
	NESTA:	No mother it s so hard getting it through the holes	" " , , '.
16	CUSTOMER:	May I try on this dress in the window	" " ?
	ASSISTANT:	I think you should use the dressing room madam	" " , .
17	JUSTIN:	Who gave you that black eye	" " ?
	KENNY:	Nobody gave it me I had to fight for it	" " ; .
18	CUSTOMER:	I d like to buy some crocodile shoes	" " '.
	ASSISTANT:	What size does your crocodile take	" " ?
19	PASSENGER:	Those people down there look just like ants	" " .
	AIR STEWARD:	They are ants we haven t left the ground yet	" " —'.
20	CAR DRIVER:	Sorry I ve killed your cat I ll replace it	" " '. '.
	OLD LADY:	But how well can you catch mice	" " ?
21	BOX OFFICE		
	GIRL:	That s the third ticket you ve bought	" " '. '.
	CINEMA-GOER:	I know a girl inside keeps tearing them up	" " ; .
22	MANAGER:	Why do you want to work in a bank	" " ?
	APPLICANT:	I understand there s money in it	" " '.
23	SNAKE-		
	CHARMER:	Careful There s a ten foot snake in that box	" " ! '- .
	PORTER:	You can t kid me snakes don t have feet	" " —' !
24	BRIDE:	Antony wake up I heard a mouse squeak	" " , ! .
	GROOM:	What do you want me to do get up and oil it	" " —?

Story Section

These are the punctuation marks: comma (,), full stop or period (.), quotation marks or inverted commas ('' '' or ' '), exclamation mark (!), question mark (?), apostrophe ('), and hyphen (-).

These stories lack their punctuation signs. Insert the correct punctuation mark in each space indicated by ☐. You may find it helpful to read the stories aloud or nearly so. It might also be useful to look through the work in the first section of this book before you begin.

1 A woman whose family kept many pets
   looked out of her window one day when
   she heard knocking at the door☐
   A boy stood there☐
   ☐Can I help you☐☐she asked☐
   ☐Not me☐☐he replied☐☐but
   there☐s a rabbit on your doorstep
   and I don☐t think he can reach the bell☐☐

2 A motorist had trouble with his car☐He called
   at a garage☐A mechanic looked at the engine☐
   ☐H☐m☐It☐ll take about £100 to get it
   purring again☐☐he said☐
   ☐Oh dear☐☐exclaimed the motorist☐
   ☐how much will it cost just to get it
   to miaow a little☐☐

3 Two birds perched on a tree not far from
an airport☐Suddenly a jet plane screamed across
the sky☐
☐Did you see that☐☐said one bird☐☐I've
never seen a bird fly as fast as that☐☐
The other bird said☐☐I bet you☐d go as fast
as that if your tail was on fire☐☐

4 Peter and Paul were friends☐They often played
together on their bikes☐Peter especially
liked to ride on his friend☐s shining new
bike☐One day Peter called for Paul☐
☐I☐m sorry☐Peter☐☐said his friend☐s
mother☐☐Paul can☐t come out this morning☐☐
☐Oh☐☐said Peter☐looking disappointed☐
Then he brightened up☐☐Can his new bike
come out instead☐☐he said☐

5 Joanna had just begun school☐and☐already☐
she thought she could read and write☐One day
her mother saw her scribbling on some paper☐
☐What are you drawing☐☐she asked☐
☐I☐m not drawing☐☐said Joanna
indignantly☐☐I am writing a letter to
Sara☐☐
☐But you can☐t write☐☐said her mother☐
☐That☐s all right☐☐said Joanna☐☐Sara
can☐t read☐☐

Can you explain the point of each story? You may like to add pictures by
the side of each story. (Look at the picture with the first story.)
There are some more stories to punctuate on the next four pages.

6 A lion and a lioness were asleep in their
cage □ much to the disappointment of a boy who
was visiting the zoo with his father □ The man
put a coin in the tape □ recorder machine □
As the boy listened to the description of the
animal □ the lion rolled over □ yawned □ then
stood up and roared loudly □
The boy □ delighted □ pointed to the still □
sleeping lioness □
He shouted □ □ Put another in the box □ Dad □ □

7 A sword □ swallower was demonstrating his
skill □ He swallowed some pins and nails □
□ Oh □ Oh □ □ scoffed the onlookers □ □ Those
aren □ t swords □ They □ re only pins and
nails □ □
□ Well □ you see □ □ said the sword □ swallower □
□ I □ m on a diet □ □

8 A young pigeon was allowed to fly out by himself
for the first time □ He just managed to get home
with his feathers bedraggled □ his tail
plucked □ and his wings limp □
□ Whatever has happened □ □ asked his mother □
□ It □ s not my fault □ □ moaned the young pigeon □
□ I flew down to see what game two girls were
playing □ □
□ What were they playing □ □ asked his mother □
□ Badminton □ □ said the young pigeon □ □ and □
before I knew where I was □ I was the
shuttle □ cock □ □

26

9 The family had been to the circus□ They all
seemed impressed by the knife□thrower except
Timothy□
□I thought he was very clever□ □said Father□
□He was no good at all□ □said Timothy□
□I don□t know how you can say that□ □said
his father□ Look at how fast and furiously
he threw those knives at the girl□ □
□But he missed every time□ □exclaimed
Timothy□

10 A competition for the biggest pumpkin was held
at a Youth Club□
A notice was put on the peg board□
□Pumpkin Contest□ □it said□
□All those interested please sign below□ □
Among the signatures was written the name
□Cinderella□ □

11 A dignified gentleman□ who did not like
children□ was enjoying a quiet read in a very
silent library□ Suddenly a class of noisy
young children came in□ They were very
excited□ and they were very noisy□
At last the dignified gentleman could stand
the noise no longer□ He called the teacher to
him□ When she returned to the class she said□
□Will you all make less noise□ That gentleman
says that he can□t read□ □
□Then he should be ashamed of himself□ □
said one girl□ □I could read when I was
only five years old□ □

12 A man was taking a stroll through the park
when a penguin suddenly appeared in front
of him□He took the penguin to the park□
keeper□and said□□I□ve found this penguin□
What shall I do□□
The keeper suggested he took the penguin to
the zoo□
The next day the park□keeper met the same man
still with the penguin□He walked up to him□
□Didn□t I tell you to take the penguin to
the zoo□□he said□
□Yes□replied the man□□and that□s what
I did yesterday□I□m taking him to the cinema
today□□

13 A policeman in the park saw a duck which had
strayed from the pool□He caught it□tied
a piece of string round its neck and led it
back to the pool□
He met two boys□They stared at him amazed□
□What do you think of that□□said one boy□
□They must have run out of police dogs□□

14 A farmer decided that his horse was over□fed
by people passing through the field□He placed
a notice on the gate□
□Please do not give this horse tit□bits□
Signed□The Owner□□
A few days later he was surprised to see
another notice on the gate below his own□
It read□□Please do not pay attention to
the above notice□Signed□The Horse□□

28

15 A teacher was telling her class the story of
Noah and his ark☐They were very impressed at
the thought of all the animals going into the
ark two by two☐
☐What do you think they did when they were
all in the ark☐☐asked the teacher☐
There was silence☐
☐All right☐What do you think Noah did☐☐she then asked☐
☐Fished☐☐said one girl☐
☐What☐☐exclaimed a young fisherman☐
☐With only two worms☐☐

16 A lion was roaring his way across the jungle
when he saw a wild pig☐He roared☐
☐Who is the king of the jungle☐☐
☐You are☐☐squeaked the pig☐
The lion went on his way and met a deer☐
He roared☐☐Who is the king of the jungle☐☐
☐You are☐☐answered the deer☐
Once more the lion went on his way☐
He came upon an elephant☐He roared☐
☐Who is the king of the jungle☐☐
The elephant picked the lion up with his
trunk☐swung him round☐and threw him to
the ground☐The lion picked himself up☐
☐All right☐All right☐☐he said☐
☐There☐s no need to get mad because you
don☐t know the answer☐☐

Answers

Now test yourself (capitals and full stops) (page 7)
A 1 The dog barked when the burglar approached. 2 As he passed through the laser beam the gates shut. 3 No one knew the answer. 4 The horseman was lost in a cloud of dust.

B The prized mascot of an American regiment in Germany was a buffalo named Cross-eyes. They kept it in a large cage. A British regiment felt sorry for the animal. One morning the buffalo disappeared. In its place was an Oxo cube.

C There was an old man of Kildare, / Who climbed into a very high chair; / When he said, "Here I stays, / Till the end of my days." / That immovable man of Kildare.

Now test yourself (commas) (page 9)
A 1 The farther he travelled, the more weary he became. 2 I will go, but you will stay here. 3 The deeper you dig, however, the wetter the ground becomes. 4 Before the fire brigade arrived, the house was burnt to the ground. 5 First, I would like to know which school you attend. 6 Yes, I am much better today. 7 Jane Powell, my best friend, will be there to meet me. 8 Stand in front of me, Jonathan, and let me take a good look at you. 9 The prisoner, wounded though he was, managed to escape. 10 There are 52,678,391 people living in the country.

B 1 Manchester, Bonn and Oslo are towns. 2 Chess, lacrosse and tennis are games. 3 Ant, earwig and termite are insects. 4 Barometer, camera and computer are instruments. 5 Zinc, iron and tungsten are minerals.

Now test yourself (question marks and exclamation marks) (page 13)
A 1 Where did you find the owl with the broken wing? 2 Don't make me laugh! 3 You are the most remarkable person I have ever met! 4 Am I invited to your party? Do you really want me to come! 5 Will you come to me immediately? I said immediately! 6 Oh! Why did you creep so quietly up to me? You are frightening! 7 Dear! Dear! Why don't you hit the nail instead of my finger? 8 Goodness gracious me! Look at the time! Shouldn't we be going? 9 Knock! Knock! Who's there? 10 What are you doing? That hurts! 11 Where are you hiding? Come out at once? 12 Now! Now! You have forgotten!

Now test yourself (pages 22–3) (Check your rating.)

Count ten points for each correct answer. Minus a point in each answer for any mistakes you have made. You would get 240 points for all-correct answers.

1 "Don't pull faces at the bull-dog." "But, mother, he began it!"
2 "What can you give me for my flat feet?" "What about a foot-pump!"
3 "Why are you rolling the potato patch?" "I'm trying to grow mashed potatoes."
4 "What has happened to this egg?" "I don't know, madam, I only laid the table."
5 "Do you serve ducklings here?" "We serve anybody, sir. Sit down!"
6 "How do you make a sausage roll?" "That's easy! Just turn it over and over."
7 "How do you know your teacher loves you?" "She puts wee kisses next to each sum I do. There!"
8 "Doctor, I feel as limp as a pair of curtains." "You had better pull yourself together then."

9 "I don't like the look of that codfish. It's bad!" "If it's looks you want, why not buy a goldfish?"

10 "Your brother is very small, isn't he?" "Well, vicar, you see, he is only my half-brother."

11 "This is a second-hand shop, isn't it?" "Yes." "That's lucky! Please fit one on my watch."

12 "So you've lost your dog. Why don't you advertise?" "Don't be silly! My dog can't read."

13 "Well, Jean, how do you like school?" "Closed!"

14 "I've changed my mind." "Does the new mind work any better?"

15 "Have you filled the salt cellar yet, Nesta?" "No, mother, it's so hard getting it through the holes."

16 "May I try on this dress in the window?" "I think you should use the dressing room, madam."

17 "Who gave you that black eye?" "Nobody gave it me; I had to fight for it."

18 "I'd like to buy some crocodile shoes." "What size does your crocodile take?"

19 "Those people down there look just like ants." "They are ants — we haven't left the ground yet."

20 "Sorry I've killed your cat. I'll replace it." "But how well can you catch mice?"

21 "That's the third ticket you've bought." "I know; a girl inside keeps tearing them up."

22 "Why do you want to work in a bank?" "I understand there's money in it."

23 "Careful! There's a ten-foot snake in that box." "You can't kid me! Snakes don't have feet!"

24 "Antony, wake up! I heard a mouse squeak." "What do you want me to do — get up and oil it?"

Rating Chart

230 to 240: Excellent. Any mistakes you have made are probably due to carelessness.

215 to 230: Very good. Notice your mistakes and avoid this kind of mistake in the future. A little more practice and you will gain confidence.

165 to 215: Fair. Find out why you are making the mistakes and check the work pages which could help you to avoid them.

Below 165: Look carefully at the punctuation in the books you are reading. Try reading aloud and notice how the punctuation marks help you.

ISBN 0 340 52723 4

This Headway edition first published 1990

Second impression 1991

Printed in Great Britain for the educational publishing division of
Hodder & Stoughton Ltd, Mill Road, Dunton Green, Sevenoaks, Kent by
CW Print Group, Loughton, Essex.